Through The Years

Jan. 2011

To Betty –
My "new" good friend.
Arlene

Through The Years

Arlene Christen Lockard

Library of Congress Control Number: 2010910255
ISBN: Hardcover   978-1-4535-2811-2
                  Softcover   978-1-4535-2810-5
                  Ebook   978-1-4535-2812-9

To order additional copies of this book, contact:
Xlibris Corporation
1-888-795-4274
www.Xlibris.com
Orders@Xlibris.com
79500

CONTENTS

DEDICATION

This book is dedicated to my sons, Scott, David and Ricky, who were the inspiration for many of the poems included here. Also to my late husband, Oscar, who believed in me even when I didn't!

Acknowledgement is also made to two of my school teachers, Mrs. Theresa Keefe (Case Elementary School) and Miss Alice Swaim (East High School) who were instrumental in my earliest poetic efforts.

Acknowledgements

My gratitude to my granddaughter, Sarah Lockard, who did the cover illustrations as well as the black and white interior images. Not only is she a very talented artist, but she's an amazing young woman and I'm proud to be her "Grandy".

My thanks also to my many long-time friends and classmates who "through the years" have said I should write a book. I hope they're satisfied!

A Friend

Though you may travel all alone
Right to the world's end,
You could not even make a start
If you had not a friend.

You do your best, you give your all,
Your work others commend,
But you could not have done a thing
Without an urging friend.

Who brought comfort to you when
You felt but dark despair?
Who gave of himself to you,
Your heartache tried to share?

Who helped you down that Road of Life,
Defeat at every bend?
You needed words of praise, but most,
You needed just a friend.

Who cheered you up when you felt low?
Who made a man of you?
Who overlooked your many faults?
True friends are very few.

For in this world of many tears,
Of sorrows long and sad,
All things are not so dark and bleak
If just one friend you've had.

Life's Winter

Today I thought when I awoke,
"How wonderful is Life!"
Its beauty heretofore had been
Outweighed by petty strife.

The sunlight filled my shabby room
And outlined it in gold;
Designs of crystal on the panes,
The air was fresh and cold.

And from my window I could see
The earth in winter dressed.
The snow was on the window sill,
The bird was in its nest.

But, though the flowers and the trees
Had fallen fast asleep
And long been covered by a soft,
White blanket cold and deep,

I knew inside that soon this ice
Would melt with the coming Spring.
And so it is with Life when troubles
Often darkness bring.

But soon the clouds are parted
With the quickness of a knife;
And so we find that after all
How wonderful is Life!

Shop Early!

Each year as Christmas rolls around
I'm filled with dire confusion.
To do my shopping early
Is indeed a mere illusion.

The pushing mobs, the crowded stores,
The snow upon the ground
Make walking much more difficult,
Gifts harder to be found.

My list looks like a tax return.
Not knowing any more
What present should I buy for whom,
I grope from store to store.

With money spent, and patience too
I find I've missed Aunt Shirley.
So take a tip from me and do
Your Christmas shopping early!

Mothers

Many authors love to tell

About their mothers. Good and well.

But, if I may add something small—

I think my Mom's the best of all!

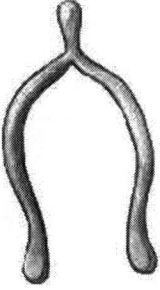

Wishbones

Some people find wishbones a source of delight:

Alas! I confess I do not.

For if the poor chicken had gotten its wish

It wouldn't have wound up in the pot!

Self-Made Man

You chide me with the claim that I
Let opportunity go by.
We mold our future you proclaim.
We fashion our defeat or fame.

But I insist it's all a plan
Unchangeable by mortal man.
Why struggle with the powers of fate
Which take eons to contemplate?

Plan now for future times, you say.
Anon tomorrow's yesterday.
In your perspective, can you tell
How long on earth I'll chance to dwell?

No, I shall live life day by day
And greet tomorrow, come what may.
If filled with love each hour can be,
Then this to me is Destiny.

Love of Life

Some there are
Who, from their birth,
Must leave their mark
Upon the earth.

Ambition burns
Within their breast
Filling them
With deep unrest.

Others are,
While years are fleeing,
Happy and content
Just being.

Trust

Where there's no trust there cannot be

A lasting peace of mind.

Where there's no faith there is no love—

The strong, enduring kind.

View from a Plane

The clouds below seem so unreal—
An endless bedspread of chenille.
The patchwork farms of green and gold:
A quilt of beauty to behold.

Below the parched, cracked landscape lies
Like upper crusts of apple pies.
The cities offer their delights—
A million Christmas trees by night.

D.D.S.

Here's to the dentist
The blood-chilling dentist,
The nerve shattering dentist,
That doctor in white.

For tho' we lament him,
At times we resent him,
We can't circumvent him
And still keep our bite.

Here's to the dentist—
The hair-raising dentist,
The chair-raising dentist
Who stands drill in hand.

So here's to the dentist!
Three cheers for the dentist!
(Twice a year for the dentist
Is all we can stand.)

The Return of the Prodigal Son

A youth of modern day there lived
Who, though half-grown, avowed
To meet the challenge of his Age
And stand out in the crowd.

He yearned to strike out on his own,
His mind on freedom bent;
For he'd had his fill of easy life,
Of the "establishment".

And so he left his father's house,
He grew his sideburns long.
On tambourine or on guitar
He sang his protest song.

He walked the crowded city streets,
He slept at night in slums.
He did his thing, he smoked his pot.
His meals at times were crumbs.

His money dwindled quickly,
(For the price of freedom's high.)
And on a college campus once,
He thought he'd surely die

When bullets whizzed around his head
And chaos reigned supreme.
The uniformed policemen's clubs
Seemed terrifying dreams.

He saw his father's loving face
Before him in his sleep.
And so began the homeward trek,
For family roots grow deep.

No fatted calf awaited him;
No ring to grace his hand;
No loving arms embraced him;
There played no welcoming band.

And when the door swung open
How his heart leapt in his breast!
Instead of father's countenance,
An unfamiliar guest.

"How many times he wrote you,
For you caused him much distress,
But all the letters came back
Marked 'No forwarding address.'

His last thoughts, they were of you."
(Here he sadly shook his head.)
"You just returned too late, my boy.
You see, your father's dead."

God Smiled at Me

God must have smiled at me one day
When He looked down on earth
And saw how all alone I was;
My life had little worth.

Into His Book of Life He wrote
An extra page or two.
He rearranged my destiny—
I fell in love with you.

Each day has greater meaning now,
The brighter side I see.
Each night I thank the Lord above
For smiling down on me!

Engagement Ring

Diamond ring upon my hand
Shining brightly, looking grand.
More than just a jewel for finger,
You brought changes that will linger.

Symbol of unending love
Sanctified by Him above.
Sign of our intent and pride
To face the future side by side.

Letting the wide world know
That through life we want to go
Together always, sharing all;
Answering Wealth's or Poverty's call.

May the hand that placed you there
Be near to stroke my silver hair;
When life has made us gray and old,
May that same hand be mine to hold.

Looking at your jewels in gold,
All these things do I behold.
May you stay unscratched, unbent
As the love you represent.

How Well I Know Thee, Love

I know your hair, your eyes, your walk,
Your smile, your laugh, your voice.
I know whene'er you hesitate
What is to be your choice.

When troubles cloud your happiness
I know I best be still
And wait until the mood has passed,
As pass it quickly will.

I know just when to share your joy
And when to hold my tongue.
I know just how you'll look with age,
Though now you're strong and young.

I also know I'll share your life
And with you I'll turn gray.
I know I'll love you just as much
As I love you today.

Little Stranger

Parents standing side by side
Gazing fondly, full of pride
At the new-born baby there,
Sleeping soundly, without care.

Little baby, soft and sweet,
You make Mother's life complete;
Tiny bundle, bouncing boy,
You're your Daddy's pride and joy.

Nothing else could mean so much
As your slightest sound or touch.
They'll watch and wait for quite a while
Just for one, small, toothless smile.

Object of abundant love,
You're a blessing from above
Come to dwell in home and heart;
Taking over from the start.

Little baby, fast asleep,
Unaware how warm, how deep
Is your parents' love for you,
Till someday you're a parent too.

Children

Children cry and scream and fuss
Making nervous wrecks of us;
Shout and race throughout the house,
Soiling trousers, tearing blouse.

Leave fingerprints on all they touch;
Nothing's safe while in their clutch.
Who can bang the kitchen door
Louder than a child of four?

Quarrel over toys they own
While you're on the telephone.
Who must by the hand be led
Up the stairs and into bed?

Who's the first one in the pool,
But must be hurried off to school?
They dig for treasure, old and charred,
In their very own backyard.

They skin their elbows and their knees,
Forget to say "thank you" and "please".
Their foolish questions all the day
Cause many a mother to turn gray.

There's many who, and rest assured,
Think children should be seen, not heard.
Yes, children are a lot of bother;
Try telling this to some proud father!

New Lawn

The day was warm,
The sun was bright,
But soon it faded into night;
And still you weeded on.

The day was gray,
The sky as well,
And soon the soft, warm raindrops fell,
But still you weeded on,

By the challenge you're possessed
Till with weeds you seem obsessed.

The children came,
The children went;
With suntanned back and shoulders bent
Alas! You weeded on!

Green Thumb

The seedlings in my flower beds

Decline to raise their showy heads.

The dandelions throughout my lawn

Rejuvenate with every dawn!

Battle of the Bulge

Protesting men's fashions,

Indignant he's risen:

His trousers are tapered,

My poor husband isn't!

Environment

As mother of three healthy boys
I think I'll never stand the noise,
But when they're gone (and why deny it?)
It's harder yet to stand the quiet!

Danger Sign

Never mind the noise, dear mother,
Don't bother when they riot.
The time to check up on the kids
Is when they grow too quiet!

Grace

Every night at dinner time
With each one in his place,
My son, who's four, says "Bow your heads",
And then recites the Grace.

The baby, who can barely talk,
Must say it all again.
It sounds a little bit like this:
"God . . . food . . . Amen!"

Condensed Time

"My Mommy says I must go in",
He said with heartfelt sorrow;
"But just you wait—I'll play with you
For one whole week tomorrow!"

Dove of Peace

A snow-white pigeon perched upon
Our roof the other day;
The children grew excited
When it didn't fly away.

These words came to my mem'ry as
We stood and gazed above:
"The Heavens opened . . . the spirit of God
Descending like a dove"

Only a pigeon after all
And maybe not a dove,
But still in that brief moment
We were caught up in God's love.

Fleeting Helper

I got the answer to my wishes:
My four-year-old start drying dishes.
With greatest zeal he did this chore
And when he finished asked for more.

One week went by, when half-way through
He said, "I left a few for you."
And now that the excitement's gone
I'm washing dishes all alone!

My Husband: The Handyman

A lover of Nature, my husband, he says
That a walk in the woods will revive me;
The children come home from a hike with their Dad
Exhausted and with poison ivy!

One day he repaired my old washing machine;
(A fifteen-cent washer it needed.)
It ended up costing twelve dollars in all;
"Something must have gone wrong", he conceded.

As family barber he often becomes
A little impatient and careless;
Our boys, though so willing and happy at first,
Have a way of emerging quite hairless!

When he offers to fix things, I have to admit
I'd much rather simply ignore him,
But after we brush all the mishaps aside,
The children and I just adore him.

Accurate Measurement

Each mother's a method
All her own
For telling how much
Her children have grown.

I know my children
Are growing tall
By the height of the fingerprints
On the wall.

Sixth Grade Camp

My last sixth grader went to camp;
I tearfully packed his clothes.
He came back with a terrarium
And also a cold in the nose!

Boy's Best Friend

They say that dog is Man's best friend—
I'm sure that this is true.
When you forget to wash your hands,
They don't get mad at you.

A dog won't borrow money or
Ask for your favorite toys.
I think that boys were made for dogs
And dogs were made for boys.

There's many things a dog can do,
Like hunt or catch a ball;
And if I'm feeling lazy, why
A dog won't care at all.

I've always longed to have a dog,
But Mom says, "No soap, Son."
I guess the only dog I'll get
Is one inside a bun!

Mother's Day Remembered

Today is the day after Mother's Day,
And oh! What a change in the scene!
I was pampered and kissed
And so hard to resist;
All my wishes came true—I was queen!

But, today brought the laundry, the cleaning, the cooking;
And then, with the dishes piled high
All the children I reared
One by one disappeared.
"Back to being a mother", I sigh.

The Cost of Higher Education

My grocery and electric bills are down—

That's common knowledge.

My phone bill has quadrupled now

I have a son in college!

Vacation Time

Vacation time is drawing near;
With many plans in mind,
You want to get away from all
And leave your home behind

Maybe you plan to motor South
Or up to Hudson Bay;
It makes no difference where you go,
Just so you get away.

You swim or fish, you get a tan,
Or in the shade you doze;
Vacation time goes quickly
And it's drawing to a close.

Somehow it seems that always,
No matter where you roam,
The best part of vacation
Is the welcome sight of home.

Lost Romance of Youth

A postage stamp stuck upside-down

Meant "love" when we were lasses.

But now it simply means that I

Forgot to wear my glasses!

Regrets

The saddest part of vacation

Isn't the fact that it's over.

All things end.

It's the memory of the plans, the anticipation

And the excursions skipped for lack of time.

The saddest part of life

Isn't death.

All things die.

It's the memory of plans, the anticipation

And the unfulfilled dreams.

Foresight

I'll not have eyes to see your tears
Nor voice to query, "Why?"
I will not smell the flowers
Heaped around me when I die.

The praises flowing easily,
That fall around my head,
Will not be given second thought
By me when I am dead.

So save your mourning colors,
All your loving words and tears;
And love me less when I am gone
And more while I am here.

Solace

When I am old, don't weep for me
For I shall not be sad;
Don't pity me, nor dull the thoughts
Of happiness I've had.

Don't mourn for all my silver hair,
Nor stretch for me the truth;
I'll know the joy of wisdom then,
The price of which is youth.

Christmas Exchange Gifts

"It doesn't fit."

"It doesn't match."

"Wrong color." "Such expense!"

She's the kind

Who fault would find

With myrrh and frankincense.

My Prayer for Peace

In these sad times, dear Lord, I pray
To let this fighting cease;
Let not so many lives be lost—
Once more let there be peace.

While all is quiet over here
We may not be aware
Of all the bloodshed, death and strife
That's constant over there.

Not conscious of the many men
With families and wives
Who've died not even questioning
The shortness of their lives.

Of younger boys, who've never known
The wonder of first love;
Whose only hope lies in the prayers
They offer You, above.

They look to You for guidance and
The hope that they may live
A normal, long and happy life;
They beg You to forgive

Their selfishness for asking
To still live when all is done.
Oh Lord, please bring us peace again
And bless them—every one.

God's Love

Can we poor mortals understand
Or even start to know
The reasons why God made the earth,
And why he loves it so?

It was not meant for us to know
For if we did, I fear
The knowledge of our sinful ways
Would bring remorse and tears.

How patient are our Father's ways!
How mighty is His love!
With mercy and with gentleness
He watches from above.

There are so many kinds of love;
Like His there is but one.
His love for us so great He gave
His precious, Holy Son.

Raise up your voice in grateful prayer,
Sing praise to Him above,
Who blessed our small, unworthy souls,
With His eternal love.

Reunion

They've reached the end of
Their mortal life,
That dear old man and
His beloved wife.

With aching hearts
And tears that flow
We sadly whisper,
"There they go."

A loved one waits
On the distant shore,
A loved one who
Passed on before;

Into his arms
Walk Dad and Mom
As he joyfully whispers,
"Here they come."

I.R.A.

The time has come to reap the fruits
Of years of toil and strife;
The chance to benefit from all
The sacrifice of life.

The long-awaited time to rest
From tedious routine;
To put away the tools of trade,
A time for change of scene.

Somewhere between your birth and death
And youth so quickly spent
Come golden days: man's brief reward;
It's called *RETIREMENT*!

Wake

However do you say "goodbye"
To those you leave behind?
What words impart to touch each heart
To keep you on their mind?

You live your life, you laugh, you love,
You do your best to smile
So when you're gone your mem'ry lives on
For just a little while.

Football Logic

When overpaid players can't score in the clutch,
Forget about penalties, fumbles and such.
The remedy's simple—just take this approach:
Hold onto the players and fire the coach!

Funerals

Funerals are sad affairs
With mourning black and mumbled prayers.
Neighbors come, and friends as well,
With common bond: to say farewell.

The tears are moist on every cheek;
Some cannot find the peace they seek
To know this dear, departed one
Is happy now beyond the sun.

Some there are who cannot cry,
Who in their hearts must bid goodbye
To friend or loved one lying there
Apart from this sad world of care.

Someone put it, wisely said,
"Cry for the living, not the dead.
She's happy now, she has no fears
For God will wipe away her tears.

"It's we on earth must daily strive
For ways and means to stay alive.
She knew the while her time drew near
That God would wipe away her tears."

Revised and Edited

The Yuletide has again arrived.
Tho' once such pleasure I derived
From sending cards to friends and kin,
In recent years my joy's worn thin.

My list reflects so many holes—
Divorce and death each takes their tolls.
Someday will I be sadly missed
When crossed from someone's Christmas list?

Of Me I Sing

I lately took note
That I'm missing the boat;
I'm not even making the scene.
May sound like sour grapes,
But on records or tapes
I have never heard songs for *Arlene.*

On fiddle or flute—
It needn't be cute;
(I hope you can see what I mean.)
It's perfectly clear
What I'm longing to hear
Is simply a song for *Arlene.*

Men all go crazy
Just singing of *Daisy*
And *Gigi* can drive them insane.
What woman could blame me?
I'm jealous of *Amy;*
I'm thinking of changing my name.

They get weak in the knees
When they sing of *Louise,*
Irene they keep telling goodnight.
Jean, Mary and *Sue*
And *Sweet Adeline* too
Are a source of melodic delight

You have *Sweet Lorain*
And *Lili Marlene,*
Dolores and *Alice Blue Gown,*
You hear *Nola* and *Lola*
On the old Victorola;
Elvira and *Sweet Georgia Brown.*

I hate to complain
And I'm not being vain,
But I'm feeling unsung and unseen.
To answer my prayer—
Won't someone somewhere
Come up with a song for *Arlene?*

The Last Laugh

You say that I'm behind the times,
My poems read like nursery rhymes;
I could give up and say, "So what's the use?"
But somehow I'll keep right on plying
My old-fashioned versifying;
I could become another Mother Goose!

I Wonder . . .

Did Jesus have a Grandma
To hold him on her knee;
To bake him cookies, bring him toys,
Rock him tenderly?

And did she know
He'd someday die to take away our sin?
If Jesus had a Grandma,
Then how proud she must have been!

Goodbye Yellow Ribbons

Americans rally
And pass on the spark,
But to me yellow ribbons
Fall short of the mark.

I can't comprehend how
They got so empowered
When yellow was always
The hue of the coward.

Why not purple for royalty,
True blue for loyalty,
Red, white and blue for our flag?
White denotes purity,
Orange for security
Or a black mourning banner to wag?

But wash them and press them
And fold them away
For they may come in handy
On some future day

When some other small nation
Won't cease and desist
And the U. S. must give them
A slap on the wrist.

Will the day ever come
When the whole world is free
And the "I" and the "You"
Are replaced by the "We"?

The ribbons need never
Again be unfurled
When true brotherly love
Is embraced by the world.

To My Friend

Of all of life's possessions
There is one that stands alone;
It is precious, it is fragile,
Yet more solid than a stone.

Friendship is this rare commodity,
The vital supplement;
And it takes a lot of nurturing
And lots of love well spent.

If you happen to be blessed with friends
Then you know what I mean.
Neither illness, time nor distance
Can conspire to intervene.

Not a single angry act nor word
Should separate two friends,
For hearts and feelings take too many
Wasted years to mend.

But take the time to speak your heart
Just as you speak your mind.
I'm glad to have a friend like you—
A generous, caring kind!

My Prayer for You, My Prayer for Me

God grant to you the will to cope,
To persevere and not lose hope.
God grant you sunshine, not despair
And pain no more than you can bear.

Accept the wisdom of God's plan
And know your life is in His hands;
Each day a blessing from above,
Surrounded by the ones you love.

I pray for guidance every day,
That God will help me find my way
And give me strength so I may do
The things I have to do for you.

By hope and love may I be led,
With patience for the days ahead.
Please make me fit to meet the test,
So our last days may be our best.

Farewell, Friend

Did you feel the sun on your face today:
Today, the day you passed away?
Did the breeze that stirs the treetops now
Kiss and cool your fevered brow?

Does your spirit hover somewhere near?
Do you hear the sighs, can you see the tears?
Did you know that you were at the end?
I pray you rest in peace, my Friend.

Give Me Something from Your Closet

When you wonder what to give me,
Don't rush to the nearest store.
If you want something to give me,
Open up your closet door.

From our closets come our treasures—
Gathered singly o'er the years.
There we hide our secret longings:
There we hide our secret tears.

Projects of our lives, unfinished,
Bits and pieces of our past
Weave the fabric of our being,
Make us who we are at last.

Choose among forgotten treasures,
That with which you deign to part.
Give me something from your closet:
From the closet of your heart.

Foliage Folly

In most situations I know what to do;
With house plants I'm not to be trusted.
My prayer plant is now an agnostic, alas
My aluminum plant has just rusted.

Tho' usually calm and efficiently cool,
By flora I'm just disconcerted.
My peace lily's grown downright hostile and now
The wandering Jew has converted!

A Lesson in Hope

My attention was diverted by
A group of kids one day;
They laughed and chided noisily,
These boys and girls at play.

They ran and jumped, they skipped and walked,
As children always do.
And not far off a little girl
Stood watching all this too.

At first I wondered why she didn't
Join the children's race;
And then I noticed on her leg
The heavy, silver brace.

She couldn't play like other girls—
Jump rope or hide-and-seek,
But had to stand and watch instead,
Withdrawn and somewhat meek.

I thought, "How bitter she must be!
She's missing all the fun;
The others just don't know she's there,
This lonely, little one."

Somehow my heart went out to her
And tears came to my eyes,
For she was smiling happily—
Her face though young, so wise.

I learned a lot that afternoon,
My outlook, too, has grown;
It's sharing others' happiness
Wherein we find our own.

Mr. Touchdown U.S.A.

A boy not very old in years,
Yet aged in thought and view,
Took one last moment to recall
A memory or two.

A different colored uniform
He'd worn in by-gone days,
When once upon the football field
He'd won his classmates' praise.

Into his mind there came the cheer
Of "fight and never yield."
These very words now came to life
Upon war's battlefield.

Although a day ago he'd yearned
To be back home, have fun,
He knew it could not be until
This "football game" was won.

What Is Time?

What is time? The clock upon the wall?
The seasons Winter, Spring and Fall?
A mark that no one can erase?
A chance to sit and stare in space?

It's precious as the finest gold.
It's always new, but never old.
It's often wasted, more than thought.
Though badly needed, can't be bought.

What is time? A thing that's said to fly?
That can't be seen, but marches by?
Though consumed, it's seldom tasted.
So live! Let not an hour be wasted.

The Wise Choice

One day, to pacify my woes,
I bought a Bible and a rose.
They both brought comfort to my sight:
The Bible, peace—the rose, delight.

The flower opened further still;
The room with fragrance it did fill.
It was so beautiful that day,
But soon it withered fast away.

The Bible, still upon my shelf,
Brought new hope to my soul and self.
Its strength it gave for many years;
And helped to banish doubts and fears.

So heed this tale and in your plight
Let not the fleeting dim your sight,
But choose instead the lasting thing
And not the one that takes to wing.

Death

To the very young Death is
A very distant thing.
They do not understand such words
As "Death" or "Suffering".

To those in love or newly wed,
Death means just dread and sorrow
To think that those so glad today
May be alone tomorrow.

But to the old with life behind,
Who do not fear the end,
To them alone does Death become
A sympathetic friend.

The Futility of Grief in Spring

Though a thousand woes torment me,
Tell me how can I despair
When robins sing and all around me
Earth and grass scents fill the air?

As music soothes the savage creature,
Like an unguent to my soul,
I surrender to your beauty;
Touch me Spring and make me whole!

Through tears I see the sunlight streaming
Through the window of my room.
All my sorrows are defeated—
They must wait for Winter's gloom.

Imagination

When life becomes a weary bore,
You're living in the days of yore:
Use imagination!

When plans are crushed, things look so gray
You cannot face another day:
Use imagination!

A little dreaming never hurts—
It puts your mind at ease.
And if life isn't what you'd like,
In dreams it's as you please.

When tired of the beaten track,
Close your eyes and settle back:
Use imagination!

ARLENE CHRISTEN LOCKARD

To a Soldier's Sweetheart

A letter serves to cheer my heart,
To ease my mind while we're apart.
Though in this matter I've no choice,
I'd so much rather hear your voice
And hold your hand and know you're here,
But till then, keep on writing, Dear.

Gone, But Not Forgotten

Gone: the way she once said Grace.
Gone: the ever-smiling face.
Gone: the hymns and songs of praise
Reserved not just for Sabbath days.
Gone: and in their place instead—
Tears, because our Mother's dead.

Through the Years

Old friends gathered 'round the table;
(At least the ones who still are able.)
Meeting for a meal, a chat;
Having fun, but more than that,

Sharing precious memories
Of school days and the "used to be's".
Our talk was once of expectations—
Now it's tests and medications!

Reluctantly we're on our way
With plans to meet another day.
These friends so cherished and so dear
Have been my anchor through the years.

Edwards Brothers,Inc!
Thorofare, NJ 08086
09 September, 2010
BA2010252